A Stepping-Stone Book

INSECTS
in ARMOR
A Beetle Book

by ROSS E. HUTCHINS

Illustrated with photographs
by the author

Parents' Magazine Press—New York

595.76
H

CONTENTS

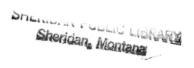

The hard, shield-like front wings of the beetle fit down
over the hind wings, when the insect is at rest. This is
the large rhinoceros beetle of the southern United States.

Chapter I

BEETLES, INSECTS IN ARMOR

Most of us know what beetles look like. They are
very common, and live in all sorts of places. Some kinds
are seen on plants. Others run about on the ground. Still
others often fly to bright lights at night. Many kinds
bore into solid wood.

Beetles are hard-bodied insects, usually dark brown or
black, but some are brightly colored. Like most flying
insects, they have two pairs of wings, but the front pair
is hard, like a shield, or armor. The shield-like front
wings are called *elytra* and do not look like wings at all.
The back pair is thin and transparent and, when the beetle
is not flying, they are folded under the front pair.
When the insect is not flying, the front wings fit tightly
down over the thin back wings to protect them. Like all
other insects, beetles have three pairs of legs. Some
beetles can run very fast.

Beetles are called *Coleoptera* by scientists. The word
comes from Greek and means "sheath wing." There are
about 275,000 kinds of beetles in the world. More than
25,000 kinds are found in North America.

Beetles vary greatly in size. The goliath beetle of Africa, for example, is nearly six inches long and has a very heavy body. Other beetles are so tiny that they are hard to see without a magnifying glass.

A typical beetle has four steps, or stages, in its life history. The adult, winged beetle lays eggs that hatch into *larvae*. (One is called a *larva*.) Beetle larvae are often called grubs. The bodies of some kinds are curved like a "C". They are usually white and have soft, tender

The larvae of many beetles are white and curved in half-circles. This beetle grub lives in the ground.

The bodies of some beetle larvae are hard and segmented, or jointed. This is the larva of a ground beetle.

bodies. Most kinds feed and grow slowly, shedding their skins several times. The skin of a beetle larva does not stretch as human skin does, to allow for increase in size. Instead, the skin gradually becomes too tight and must be shed or *molted*. After each molt, the larva is slightly larger than it was before. That is the way it grows.

Some beetles spend only a few weeks in the larval stage, while others may spend several years. When fully grown, these larvae change into *pupae*. (One is called a *pupa*.) Pupae do not eat. In time, these pupae shed their skins and become adult beetles. The winter may be passed in any one of the four stages. However, only a few kinds live over the winter in the egg stage.

Since beetles pass through four stages—egg, larva, pupa, and adult—they are said to have *complete* life histories. Their development is like that of butterflies, moths, bees, or ants.

Beetles eat all sorts of plant and animal materials. Some kinds capture and eat other insects, while others live on dead animals or on stored foods such as dried peas and beans. A number of beetles live and feed in ponds and streams.

Beetles have strong jaws, which they use to bite and chew hard materials such as wood or the tough shells of nuts. The chewing mouth parts of the weevils—one kind of beetle—are at the tips of slender snouts. This makes it possible for them to feed in deep holes or cavities.

Most beetles are harmless to man, but many are most destructive pests. These include the cotton boll weevil, the Japanese beetle, the Mexican bean beetle, among many others.

The eggs of beetles are usually laid where their larvae will feed. These eggs were laid on a leaf by a leaf-eating beetle.

The antennae of some beetles are slender and thread-like. Others, such as this striped June beetle, have strange, leaf-like antennae.

Chapter 2

THE WOOD BORERS

Beetles of many kinds bore through solid or decayed wood, often causing damage to trees or to lumber or wood products. Usually it is the larvae or grubs that live in the wood, but the adults of some beetles also live in and bore through wood.

The Long-Horned Borers
    These may be small or large, but all have very long *antennae,* or feelers. In some kinds the antennae are

The antennae of many beetles are thread-like like those of this darkling beetle.

9

Adult long-horned beetles have very long antennae. Some kinds make squeaking sounds when picked up.

much longer than their bodies. That, of course, is why they are called long-horned beetles. They lay their eggs in the bark of dead or living trees and their larvae or grubs tunnel through the wood or beneath the bark. These grubs are round and look like caterpillars. They have strong jaws used for tunneling through the hard wood. A person who sleeps in an old log cabin can sometimes hear, late at night, the sounds made by the grubs as they cut away the wood with their jaws. Often flooring and lumber are badly damaged by boring grubs.

The larvae of long-horned beetles bore in wood. Here a twig has been split open to show one of the borers and its tunnel.

A long-horned beetle has powerful jaws used for biting or for cutting through hard wood.

Some kinds of beetles spend only one year in the grub stage, but a few kinds may spend as long as seventeen years before becoming adults.

One of the more unusual long-horned borers is the twig girdler that lays its eggs near the tips of living branches of hickory, apple, elm, and some other trees. Before laying her eggs, the female gnaws a neat groove around the twig near its base. This kills the twig, and after a while it breaks off and drops to the ground.

The twig girdler cuts a groove around a twig, then lays eggs in it. Her larvae bore in the dead twig.

This twig was split open to show how a woodpecker drilled a hole in it to capture a long-horned beetle grub.

There the grub completes its growth in the dead twig and becomes an adult beetle.

Some long-horned beetles are very large, often over two inches long. Long-horned beetles nearly six inches long live in the jungles of South America.

While most of the common kinds are brownish in color, there are several that are very colorful. One of the most beautiful is the splendid long-horn that is colored with bright shades of metallic green and bronze.

A few kinds make clicking sounds by rubbing one part of their bodies against another part. This way of making sounds is called *stridulation*.

Metallic wood borer larvae have flattened bodies. The front end is enlarged.

The Metallic Wood Borers

The larvae or grubs of these beetles bore just under the bark of living or dead trees. It is easy to tell them from the grubs of long-horned borers. Metallic wood borer grubs have flattened bodies with the front part enlarged. Some kinds bore in fruit trees. One of these harmful kinds is the flat-headed apple tree borer. These beetles are called metallic borers because the adults of many kinds are bright metallic green or blue.

Adult metallic wood borer beetles have oval bodies.

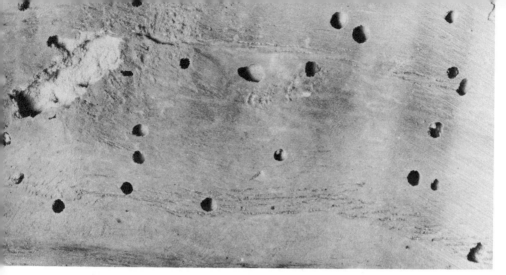

These holes in hard wood were made by powder-post beetles.

The Powder-Post Beetles

These small beetles bore holes in dry wood and large amounts of powdered wood fall out of the openings. These holes are about the size of a pencil lead, and look as if they had been made by shotgun pellets. Often furniture, wooden beams, and hardwood floors may be almost completely destroyed.

One of these beetles that lives in the West has a most unusual habit. It often bores tiny holes in lead telephone cables. This allows moisture to enter the cables, causing short circuits and interruption of

The lead-cable borer bores small holes in lead telephone cables.

telephone service. Sometimes these insects are called "short-circuit" beetles.

The Engraver Beetles

Often, when the bark is pulled off of dead trees or stumps, attractive patterns of beetle tunnels appear. These tunnels are the mines of engraver beetles. They are very small insects that bore in through the bark and then tunnel along beneath it. At intervals, the beetles lay eggs. When these eggs hatch, the grubs tunnel away, making the interesting patterns we call "engravings." After becoming adult beetles they gnaw exit holes through the bark and lay eggs in other trees.

Engraver beetles bore into trees and make tunnels beneath the bark. They lay eggs in these tunnels and the larvae bore away from the original tunnel. As they feed and grow larger, their tunnels increase in size.

15

Chapter 3

THE SCARAB TRIBE

These are heavy-bodied beetles. Some are small, some large. Many scarab beetles feed on plants, but the grubs of others, such as the tumblebugs, feed on animal dung. If you look closely at a scarab beetle you will find that the last segments, or joints, of its antennae are enlarged and plate-like. There are many kinds of these beetles and they are found in almost all parts of the world. Some are serious pests of forests, orchards, and lawns.

In ancient Egypt scarab beetles were believed to be symbols of eternal life. Many of them, carved from jade and other semi-precious stones, have been found in ancient Egyptian tombs.

The May Beetles

During warm evenings in spring we often see beetles buzzing about bright lights. Now and then one of these insects alights and we can see that it is about an inch long and brown in color. These are May beetles, but some people call them "June bugs." There are many different

May beetles are common almost everywhere.

kinds and they are found almost everywhere. Their
larvae, called white grubs, live in the ground, feeding
on the roots of plants. Sometimes there are so many of
them that lawns are damaged. The adult beetles come out
of the ground in spring and eat the leaves of trees.

Japanese Beetles

Many of our most destructive insect pests have been
accidentally brought into this country. One of these is
the Japanese beetle, a native of Japan, that was first
discovered in New Jersey in 1916. Since that time it has
spread into many other states. It eats flowers and the

17

The Japanese beetle is a serious pest.

leaves of trees. Its grubs live under the ground, where they damage the roots of grasses. Often lawns, golf courses, and pastures are harmed. The adult beetles are about half an inch long and metallic green.

The Rhinoceros Beetles

The males of these beetles have two horns on their heads. One horn is on the top of the head, and the other rises from the back. The females do not have horns.

Some kinds are small, but several are very large. In fact, the largest beetle found in North America is the

The largest beetle found in the United States is the giant rhinoceros beetle. This one is in flight. Note the horn on its head.

This large rhinoceros beetle lives in Panama.

giant rhinoceros beetle of the southern United States. In tropical countries there are even larger rhinoceros beetles.

The grubs of these beetles live and feed in rotting logs.

The adults are about two and one-half inches long. The males are greenish-gray with brownish spots. The female is all brown.

Even though these beetles are heavy-bodied, they often fly to lights with loud, buzzing sounds.

This giant rhinoceros beetle is found in Japan. The horn on its head is forked.

The Tumblebug Beetles

These beetles form dung into marble-sized balls which they roll about over the ground. It is quite amusing to watch one of these little beetles rolling its ball about. Sometimes two beetles work together, and they always seem to be in a great hurry. After the beetle finds a suitable place, the ball is buried and eggs are laid in it. The beetle grubs feed on the ball and eventually mature into adults.

Because of their ball-rolling habits, the ancient Egyptians regarded tumblebug beetles with reverence. The ball represented the earth which, it was believed, was rolled from sunrise to sunset. The beetle itself represented the sun, and the sharp projections from its head were the sun's rays. There are thirty segments, or joints, on the beetle's six legs and these were supposed to represent the thirty days of the month. For some strange reason, all of these beetles were believed to be males and so represented warriors. Later, in Roman times, soldiers wore rings set with stones cut in the shape of scarab beetles.

There are many different kinds of tumblebug beetles. Some make earthen cells that are stocked with dung.

A tumblebug beetle rolling a ball of dung around on the
ground.

Chapter 4

THE HUNTING BEETLES

Beetles of many kinds feed on insects and other small creatures that they capture in their jaws. Most of these beetles are of medium size and quite active. Some are very colorful. They are found almost everywhere. You may see them in fields and forests, or in city parks, or on lawns.

The Tiger Beetles

Sometimes on woodland trails you may see brightly colored beetles running along the ground. When disturbed, these beetles fly away very rapidly. Some kinds are found on beaches, where they run along on the sand. These are tiger beetles. They are well named because of their habit of capturing and eating flies and other insects during both their young and adult stages. Their jaws are long and sharp and are used to capture their insect game.

A tiger beetle has long, slender legs, well fitted for running rapidly over the ground.

Many kinds of tiger beetles are very pretty. Their bodies are of bright metallic shades of green and blue.

Above: Tiger beetles' jaws are toothed and very sharp. They are used to capture insects. Below: Tiger beetles have slender legs and can run very rapidly. Sometimes they fly.

Tiger beetle larvae are caterpillar-like. They hide
in holes in the ground with only their heads above
the surface.

    The larva of a tiger beetle is strange looking. It has
a slender body with a hump on its back. Its head is
flattened and it has sharp jaws. This larva lives in a
hole in the ground, often more than a foot deep. It
stays very quiet with its head in the opening to its
tunnel. When an ant or other small insect walks by, the
larva reaches out and grabs it with its jaws. The
captured insect is then dragged down into the tunnel and

eaten. Sharp spines or hooks on the hump of the beetle larva's back prevent it from being dragged out of the tunnel when a strong or active insect is captured.

Sometimes tiger beetle larvae are called "doodlebugs."

The Ground Beetles

These long-legged beetles usually hide under stones or old boards during the day. At night they roam about hunting for small insects. Some kinds eat cutworms and are thus helpful to the gardener. One kind even climbs up in trees where it captures webworm caterpillars.

Most ground beetles are jet-black, but some are quite colorful. One, the fiery hunter, is deep blue with rows of reddish spots on its wing covers.

Ground beetle larvae are not grub-like. Instead, they are dark-colored and slender with flattened bodies. They

This ground beetle has captured a cutworm.

A bombardier beetle squirting puffs of irritating gas from its rear end.

are usually found hiding in the same places as the adult beetles, and their food habits are similar.

The Bombardier Beetles

These unusual beetles are actually a kind of ground beetle. They are found in the same places as other ground beetles. There are several different kinds, but they all have a most unusual method of driving enemies away. When disturbed, these beetles shoot out puffs of irritating gas from their rear ends. These little puffs of gas look like smoke and make small popping sounds when shot out by the beetle. We may consider this method of defense to be a type of chemical warfare.

One common kind of bombardier beetle is easily recognized by its rust-red "neck."

The Ladybird Beetles

These attractive little beetles are familiar to almost everyone. They are less than a quarter of an inch long and oval in shape. Usually they are red or yellow with black spots, but some are black with red or yellow spots. They are often seen hurrying about on plants and leaves. Sometimes they fly. They are always searching for plant-lice, or aphids, because it is these and other small, soft-bodied insects that they eat. When a ladybird beetle finds a colony of aphids, it starts at once to eat them. However, the beetle is often driven away by ants that

Ladybird beetles are very common.

guard and care for the aphids in return for the sweet honeydew the aphids, or "ants' cows," secrete.

The larvae of these beetles remind one of tiny alligators. Their food habits are like those of the adults. Because of their food habits, they are considered to be helpful to man.

Ladybird beetles usually spend the winter as adults. Large numbers of them often gather together under leaves or piles of pine needles.

The larvae of ladybird beetles also feed on aphids.

Chapter 5

THE WATER BEETLES

Perhaps you would not expect to find beetles living underwater in ponds and streams. Yet many kinds spend their entire lives there. Even though these *aquatic,* or water-dwelling, beetles live below the surface, they must have air during their adult lives. They rise to the surface now and then for new supplies of air. Sometimes they leave the water and fly to other ponds or streams. Often they are attracted to bright lights at night. The adults of one kind, the whirligig beetle, live on the water's surface. Some water beetles live in hot springs in western states. Aquatic beetles are interesting because of their unusual habits.

The Diving Beetles

There are two types of diving beetles and they vary in size from quite small to nearly two inches in length. Their legs are long and are used like oars to propel them through the water. One kind, the predacious diving beetles, are hunters both as larvae and as adults. Predacious means that they live on small animals, including minnows. The

This is the predacious kind of water beetle.

water scavenger beetles, on the other hand, feed mostly on dead plant and animal material in the water. Only during their larval stage do they capture and eat live animals.

As we have said, all adult water beetles must have air. When the predacious diving beetles rise to the surface, they trap air under their wing covers. Often, they hang below the surface with their tails just touching the water. The water scavenger beetles, however, carry their supplies of air in thin, silvery films on the lower surfaces of their bodies.

Young water beetles, or larvae, are long and slender, and have sharp, sickle-shaped jaws used to capture game. They hide among water plants while waiting for unwary aquatic animals to approach. They are often called "water tigers."

Some water beetles insert their eggs in the stems of water plants. The water scavenger beetles lay their eggs in small cases, which are attached to the leaves of water plants or are left to float in the water.

Larval water beetles are called water tigers. They live on insects they capture in their sharp jaws. Most of the time they hide among water plants.

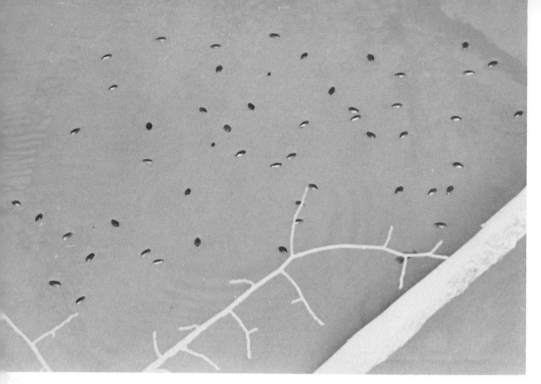

Whirligig beetles swim about on the surfaces of ponds and pools. Their larvae live in the water.

The Whirligig Beetles

Anyone who has ever explored the edges of a stream or a pond has noticed these black beetles darting about over the surface of the water. Often there are a great many of them. Some kinds have a most disagreeable odor when captured in the fingers. They feed on small insects, and sometimes fly from one pond or stream to another.

Perhaps the most unusual thing about these beetles is the fact that each eye is divided so that the upper part is above the water's surface and the lower part below it.

This enables the beetle to see both above and below the water.

These beetles' legs are short and broad, and are used like paddles to propel the insects very rapidly about over the surface. This makes them very hard to catch.

They lay their eggs on water plants.

Their larvae resemble small centipedes. They live in the water and eat tiny animals. When full grown, the larvae crawl out of the water and *pupate,* or change into pupae, in mud cells along the shore or on nearby plants.

When viewed close up it can be seen that a whirligig beetle has each eye divided so that one part is above the water and the other below.

Chapter 6

THE FIREFLY BEETLES

Many kinds of animals and plants produce light. Some mushrooms glow in the darkness and so do certain bacteria. Some one-celled animals living in warm seas flash brightly when disturbed by a passing ship. In New Zealand there are certain fungus gnat larvae that live in caves. They give off a steady glow that attracts small insects on which they feed. Best known, however, of all light-producing creatures are the fireflies, which are actually beetles.

Firefly beetles are most common in tropical lands. The cucujo beetle of the West Indies produces the most brilliant light. It has two eye-like organs on the front of its body that give off a bright, greenish light, and other organs on its belly that glow with orange light. Sometimes people use these beetles in their huts in place of candles, Sometimes the girls put them in their hair as ornaments.

Very brilliant, also, are the fireflies of Burma and Siam. They often collect in trees in large numbers, all flashing at once.

The common firefly beetle is about an inch long and has its light-making organ in its tail.

The Common Fireflies

Often called fireflies, these remarkable beetles are found in almost every part of the United States. There are about fifty different kinds, most of which produce light during their larval and adult stages.

Firefly beetles are soft-bodied and less than an inch long. Their light-making organs are in the rear portions of their bodies. Their light is considered to be "cold light" since it gives off no heat. This is unusual, because most light gives off heat—the light of the sun, or of an ordinary light bulb, for example. The firefly's light is yellowish and is produced by a substance called *luciferin.* The insect is able to turn its light off or on by controlling the amount of oxygen from the air that goes to its light organ. If you watch a firefly, you will see that it flashes its light and then "turns it off" for a few seconds.

The males have the brightest lights. They fly above

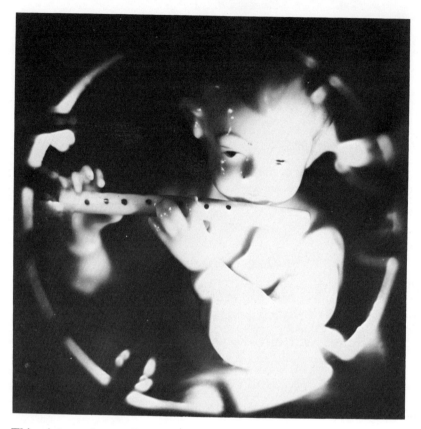

This picture of a small statue was taken by the light of several fireflies.

the ground flashing their lights now and then. The females perch in the grass or in other low-growing plants and answer the males by flashing their own lights. However, their lights are not as bright as those of the males.

Each kind of firefly has its own flash code. This is

the length of time between its flashes. Scientists have learned how to tell what kind of firefly is flying by timing the length of its flash and the time between flashes.

The larvae of fireflies are flat, jointed insects that live in damp places and feed on small insects and snails. They have light-making organs that glow in the dark, but they do not flash their lights as the adult beetles do. The larvae are called glow-worms.

The larva of the firefly is known as a glow-worm. This one is feeding on a snail.

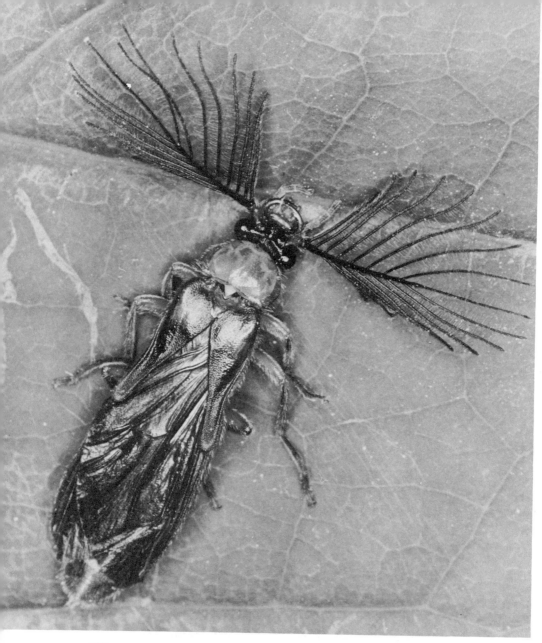

This strange-looking insect is a male phengodes or "railroad worm." Note its large, feathery antennae and short front wings.

The Railroad Worms

Closely related to the true firefly beetles are the *phengodes* beetles. They are not very common. The strange thing is that the female beetle never develops wings. She lays eggs while still in the larval, caterpillar-like stage. The male, however, is winged and has large feathery antennae.

The larvae of these beetles live in rotten logs and have light-making organs along the sides of their bodies.

The larvae of one kind of these unusual beetles is common in tropical lands. Along the sides of its body it has eleven pairs of greenish lights and a pair of red lights on its head. When crawling along, it looks like a train with flashing lights. That is why these beetles are called railroad worms.

The picture of this female phengodes beetle was taken with its own light.

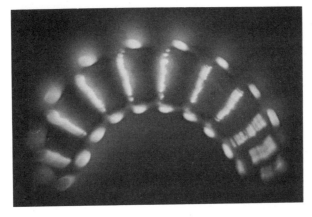

Chapter 7

THE WEEVIL CLAN

Weevils are sometimes known as "snout" beetles because
most of them have long snouts, or beaks, with the jaws
at the tip. Some of these snouts are long and slender,
almost as long as the beetle's body. They vary greatly
in size, but most kinds are not more than a quarter of
an inch long. In the tropics there are much larger
weevils.

**Weevils have their mouth parts at the tips of snouts
which are often quite long. Some weevils of tropical
countries are large. This one from Peru is more
than an inch long.**

The destructive boll weevil of cotton. This one is feeding on a cotton bud or "square."

Weevils eat a wide variety of plants. Some kinds live in dried peas, beans, and corn. Their larvae are grub-like and legless.

There are about 3,000 kinds in the United States, many of which are serious crop and garden pests.

The Cotton Boll Weevil

This well-known pest of cotton came into the United States from Mexico about 1890 and within a few years had spread over the entire cotton-growing belt of the country.

The adult weevils are about a quarter of an inch long and have slender snouts. They lay their eggs in holes in the young cotton bolls or seed pods. The larvae are grub-like. They feed in the developing bolls and damage or destroy them. The cotton boll weevil is the most serious pest of cotton.

41

The Acorn Weevil

These weevils have long, slender snouts. The female uses her snout to bore into an acorn and then lays her egg in the hole. The grub that hatches from the egg feeds on the developing nut. When mature, the grub bores out of the acorn and pupates in the soil. The adult weevil emerges the next summer.

Closely related to the acorn weevil are similar weevils that bore into hickory nuts and pecans.

The snout of the acorn weevil is nearly as long as its body. Its grubs live inside oak acorns.

Leaf-rolling weevils roll portions of leaves into tight balls and lay an egg in each one.

The Leaf-Rolling Weevil

These unusual weevils form leaves into thimble-shaped rolls. Usually only a part of the leaf is rolled up.
In each of these rolls the female lays an egg, and the grub feeds on the inner parts of the rolled-up leaf.

If the nest of a leaf-rolling weevil is cut open the egg may be seen inside.

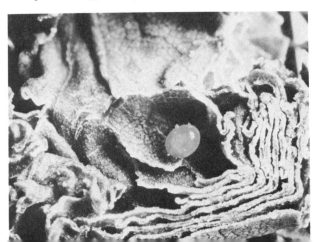

43

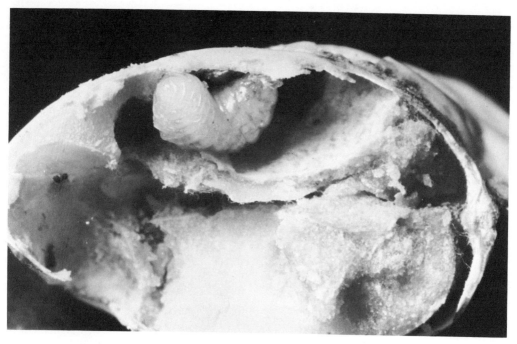

**The larvae of bean weevils live and feed inside beans.
The beans are destroyed.**

The Grain Weevils

These are tiny weevils that bore into stored rice, corn, and other grain. Both the larvae and the adults develop inside the grains. Often these small weevils are found crawling about kitchens. Usually no one suspects that they are coming from rice or other food stored on a shelf. These same weevils often cause considerable damage in large granaries.

The Sweet Potato Weevil

This is probably the world's worst insect pest of sweet potatoes. It is found in many places where these plants are grown. It is a native of tropical countries. The adult is about one-quarter of an inch long. Its head, the front part of its body, and its back are dark blue. Its legs are red. The larvae bore into sweet potato plants and also feed in the potatoes. Adult weevils also feed in the potatoes.

There may be as many as eight complete generations of these weevils in one year.

Sweet potatoes are often damaged or destroyed by sweet potato weevils.

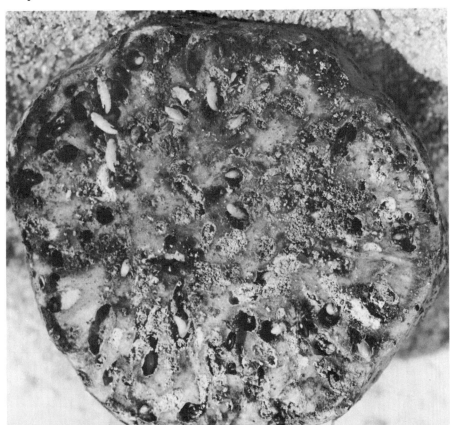

Chapter 8

SOME HARMFUL BEETLES

Beetles of many kinds often damage garden and field crops. Some of these beetles are among our most destructive pests. Many are native insects. Others were brought to the United States accidentally from foreign countries. We have already talked about some of these beetles, such as the sweet potato weevil and the Japanese beetle. Here are a few more.

The Colorado Potato Beetle

This is a native beetle that has changed its food habits. It originally ate sandbur, a wild plant found in Colorado. When early settlers came to Colorado and planted Irish potatoes, it began to eat them and became a serious pest. Since that time it has spread to all parts of the United States and to some foreign countries.

The Colorado potato beetle has an oval-shaped body, nearly half an inch long, with black and yellow stripes. The female beetles lay their clusters of eggs on the undersides of potato leaves and the reddish larvae feed on the leaves. When mature, these larvae drop to the

46

soil and pupate below the surface. A few days later the adult beetles come out.

The Mexican Bean Beetle

These small beetles belong to the ladybird beetle family but, unlike them, feed on plants. They originally lived in Mexico, but have spread to many parts of the United States. They eat the leaves of various kinds of beans, often damaging them.

The adult beetles are less than a quarter of an inch long. They are oval in shape, and yellowish or bronze in color.

Their larvae are spiny and green when newly hatched. Later they change to yellow. The inactive pupal stage is spent on the leaves where both adults and larvae feed. The adults live during the winter, hiding under trash.

The Colorado potato beetle.

Adult Mexican bean beetle and larva, both of which eat leaves.

The Click Beetles

These beetles have a most unusual habit. If you pick one up in your fingers, it snaps its body. This makes it hard to hold. This habit probably helps it to escape when it is caught in the beaks of birds. These beetles' bodies are hinged in the middle. It is the front part they snap up and down. This makes a clicking sound. If one of these beetles is placed on its back it will snap

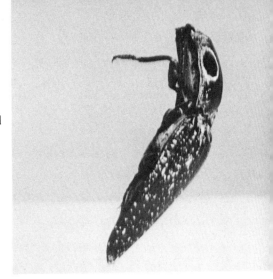

Click beetles' bodies are hinged
in the middle and may be snapped
up and down. This one, when
placed on its back, snapped itself into the air.

its body, tossing itself several inches into the air.

Click beetles' bodies are flat and range in size from
very small to more than two inches in length. They are
often seen on flowers, but may also be found under bark.
Their larvae are slender, hard-bodied, and usually brown
or yellowish. They are called wire-worms. Some kinds
live in the ground, feeding on the roots of crop plants.
For that reason they are considered to be harmful to the

This click beetle has two "eye-spots" on the front part
of its flattened body.

farmer and gardener. A few kinds live in rotting logs and stumps. One of these, known as the eyed click beetle, has two large, black eye-spots on the front part of its body.

The Tortoise Beetles

These pretty little beetles are small, hardly over one-eighth inch long. They have oval bodies and are brilliantly colored. Often they look as if they were made of gold. That is why they are sometimes called "gold bugs." Their larvae are very spiny. They eat morning glories and sweet potato plants.

Tortoise beetles eat many plants, including morning-glories. The larvae also feed on these plants.

This is called a blister beetle because some kinds
blister the skin when handled.

The Blister Beetles

These are narrow, round-bodied beetles. They are called
blister beetles because some kinds secrete a liquid
substance called *cantharidin* that causes blistering of
tender skin.

Some kinds are black, others are gray. A few kinds have
yellow stripes. Most of them are about an inch long.

Sometimes blister beetles eat flowers and other garden
plants and damage them. However, their larvae are
considered useful because they live in the ground where
they eat grasshopper eggs.

Chapter 9

SOME UNUSUAL BEETLES

Some kinds of beetles have very unusual habits. Some, such as the click beetles, have already been described. A few more are mentioned here.

The Green June Beetle

These are bright, blue-green beetles nearly an inch long. Sometimes they are called fig-eaters because, in the southern United States, they like to eat ripe figs. They often fly to bright lights with loud buzzing sounds.

The grubs live in the soil and pupate in earthen cells.

This is the pupa of a green June beetle in its earthen cell.

In time the pupa changes into a greenish beetle in its earthen cell and soon it emerges from the soil. The beetle in this picture has just changed into an adult.

Sometimes the larvae come to the surface of the ground and crawl about. But instead of crawling on their feet, they crawl along on their backs with their short legs in the air. They can do this by contracting and expanding the ringlike sections of their bodies. Why they do it no one knows.

The Stag Beetles

Sometimes these beetles are called "pinching-bugs" because of their large jaws. In some kinds, the jaws of the male are large and look like the antlers of male deer, or

Above: Male stag beetles have large jaws that remind one of antlers. As in this picture, the males often fight, using their large jaws to toss each other about. Left: The female stag beetle has much smaller jaws than the male.

stags. That is the reason for their name. The stag beetles are nearly two inches long and brown in color.

The large grubs of these beetles live and feed in rotten logs. The adult beetles sometimes fly to lights. The males frequently fight, using their large jaws to toss each other about.

The Ant-Loving Beetles

It is a strange fact that a number of tiny insects live in ant colonies where they are treated almost like pets. Among these ant "pets" are small crickets, sucking

Ant-loving beetle.

Horned passalus beetles are often called betsy-beetles. Both the adults and their grubs live and feed in rotten logs. Note the horn on this one's head.

bugs, beetles, and other insects. Some mites also live in the nests. These insects are called ant "guests" or *myrmecophiles* and they feed on food brought into the nests by the ants, or lick secretions from the ants' bodies. Beetles that live with ants are found nowhere else. They are among the strangest of all insects.

The Betsy Beetles

The proper name of these insects is horned passalus beetles, but they are usually called betsy beetles or, sometimes, bessbugs. There are four kinds, one found in the eastern United States and three in the Southwest. They are jet-black and nearly two inches long. Attached to the top of the head is a horn. Country children often attach strings to betsy-beetle horns, with match boxes attached to the strings. The beetles obligingly pull the match boxes along as if they were tiny sleds.

Betsy-beetle larvae are grub-like and live in rotten logs. The hind legs of these grubs are very small. (See the picture on page 58.) The insects use them to scrape or scratch rough patches on their bodies. In this way, a squeaking sound is produced. The adult beetles also make sounds, but in a slightly different way. They rub the bases of their wings across rough areas of their bodies. Usually a number of them live together and they are able to communicate with each other by these squeaking sounds.

A betsy-beetle pulling a match box.

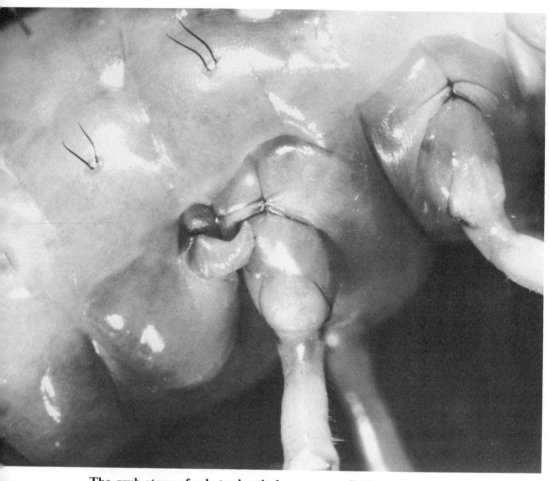

The grub stage of a betsy-beetle has very small hind legs.
The legs are fitted for scraping on a roughened patch on
the insect's body. The scraping makes a squeaking sound.
The grubs live in rotten logs.

Chapter 10

HOW STRONG IS A BEETLE?

We often see ants lifting sticks or stones that are much heavier than they are. We are always surprised that they are able to lift or carry such heavy objects. I once captured an ant that was lifting a pebble, and I weighed both the ant and the pebble. The pebble weighed fifty-two times more than the ant that had lifted it. No human could do as well.

Beetles, too, are very strong. I once made some tests using a *dynamometer,* which is a special instrument for testing strength. One of these was used to see how much a betsy-beetle could pull. I found that the beetle could pull about seven and a half times its own weight. A horse can pull only about half its own weight. The beetle, therefore, is nearly fifteen times stronger than the horse in proportion to size. In other tests, I found that a honeybee worker could pull twenty times its own weight.

Wanting to see how heavy a load a betsy-beetle could pull, I hitched one to a toy truck. In this test of strength, the beetle pulled a load weighing ninety times

In a test of strength, a betsy-beetle was able to pull a
toy truck weighing 90 times its own weight.

its own weight. This is about equal to a man pulling a
14,000-pound truck.

Beetles can also lift great weights. In one test a
long-horned beetle was able to lift 850 times its own
weight. If an elephant were as strong in proportion it
could lift a small ship.

Are beetles and other insects really stronger than
larger animals? The answer is, not really. An insect's
muscles are attached to the inside of its armor-like
body and work more efficiently. In addition, the larger

the animal, the heavier its body is in proportion to its size. Also it is the width of a muscle and not its length that determines how powerful it is. Thus scientists believe that insects are not really any more powerful than larger animals. They just seem to be.

When tested on a body-lift instrument, a long-horned beetle lifted 850 times its own weight.

INDEX

Numbers in italics indicate illustrations